EROS

SAINT JULIAN PRESS

POETRY

PRAISE for ~ *E* R O S

ÆROS

Kevin McGRATH

SAINT JULIAN PRESS
HOUSTON

Published by

SAINT JULIAN PRESS, Inc.
2053 Cortlandt, Suite 200
Houston, Texas 77008

www.saintjulianpress.com

ISBN-13: 978-0-615-72532-1
ISBN: 0-615-72532-5
Library of Congress Control Number: 2016956216

Cover art is an image of Jataka 539:
Manimekhala Saves the Mahajanaka
Myanmar, 19th Century, courtesy of Lilian Handlin.
Author photo credit, courtesy of Akos Szilvasi

CONTENTS

○

To Guy Murdo McGRATH

A quella luce cotal si diventa,
che volgersi da lei per altro aspetto
è impossibil che mai si consenta ...

Par. XXXIII, 100

EROS

O N E

A BIRD flew to the air
The great chamber was empty,
All the shadows had fled
And all the hours were in shadow.

Shadows you were
Dressed clearly like grain
Grain and thirst,
The bird of conceivable space.

I - 2

THERE are four winds about the world
That move within the human soul,
First, the strange attraction going
Between a girl and a boy.

The second takes us on in time
So that we might look back,
At the residence and procession
Of what is lost upon our way.

The third is the emptiness that
Fills up our breathing days,
As we go toward our source
Its quietness makes us more still.

The final air is that of beauty
Quick, ephemeral, always true,
The breeze that makes substantial
Everything we do not know
Song of what we cannot say.

I - 3

I LOVE that beauty shall be beautiful
And admire your lovely truth,
Ambivalence and ambiguity which
Compose the margins of a human soul:

The vivid elements and mastery
Of life imbued and balanced,
Where observation finds its pleasure
In the slow tact of your motion.

Obedient to darkness you
Possess all genius of goodness,
You are the love that finds itself
Coherent with beauty's movement,
Gracious as light itself
As it fills the world with vision.

I - 4

THE intrinsic stain of human life
Is more than a golden thread,
All boys and girls know this
Loveless dust of the world,
As they reach to hold a hand
Or catch an eye's submission:

The unbearable human soul
Clothed in a palpable body
Craving another's touch,
An oblivion of smooth warmth
And fluid of its softest tissue,
Bird of exquisite plumage.

You once yielded all desire
And promises perpetual,
Day is long and life is short
Yet the pleasure of the soul
Demands constant renewal,
Do we possess sufficient joy?

All the children of the earth
Can smile and shake a finger,
Young women might glance
As the young men stare:
But when the dust is blown
And the clothes removed
And the bird of love vanishes,
What can the lifeless soul declare
What promises are heard then?

I - 5

SO much water goes past
Flowing downstream slowly,
Rain, snow, flood, all
Make for a river's rising.

Yet when we come to a bank
Go out in our narrow boat
And bending down to taste -
How little we catch to drink.

So much current flowing
Through earth's ancient arteries,
Turning to salt experience
On reaching the big ocean.

How little touches our lips
Running out from fingers,
Yet born with a thirst we are
Always going toward water.

I - 6

DOES beauty exist in water
Can it be seen in the sky,
Or is it passing through the air
As light breaks into spring
When the wind is most on fire?

Beauty goes with timeless measure
With feet unseen to living eyes,
One slight human defect
Causes its transit to be undone
Upon a burning axle of days.

Is there beauty in a child's
Perfection of uncovered limbs,
Or in glances shot between
Young men and women's eyes
When shadow is a lucid blue?

Beauty shows herself to those
Who do not expect to stay
Beyond the effort and the anguish
That make for life without end
On a dancing floor of this place:

A sweet delicious comb of light
Of soft white generative tissue,
In whose weightless substance
Is beauty to be briefly found
In ways that we cannot say.

Beauty exists in movement
In every transient thing,
In beauty there is slowness
Brevity, lightness and
One great absence of desire.

This is a truth transparent
Equality of how time solves
Separates and divides us from
All that is coherent here,
Where beauty finds itself
Strangely wandering the world.

I - 7

IF beauty is all slowness
Our life vanishes in haste,
If we might only pause
Earthly loveliness would be
More apparent and its truth
Take on formal weight.

In stillness lies our cause
The forceful decency of life,
Hastening, we lose ourselves
And the particles of time.

On the one hand is decay
And on the other is duration,
Love is our infallible guide
As vision reveals balance:
How the human spirit weeps
Soul dripping from our eyes
As it witnesses the racing.

I - 8

FOR a short time an endless moment
Two swans swimming down a river,
Or as two gold lions pace
The shore-line of an empty coast.

So too in time these present days
When the tissue of spring is torn,
A world puts on its fiction and
Its lovely tinted new illusions.

Crimson leopards walk at night
Beneath heavy dripping trees,
As optimism - like a bird
Or certitude - flies from the moon.

May we always keep this rest
As a constant inner world,
Where marriages are only true
Renewed each day with satisfaction
And the warm river never ends.

I - 9

OF all extant beauty
Dark star without possession,
Whose lovely cruelty retreats
Covering itself inside light:
We are poured out, the river
Tells me, at this lilac time.

As you, my bride in the air
Whose currency exceeds
Sweet black cavities of night,
You and I pretend
Thinking we are discrete.

We are a music others hear
Being carried on elsewhere
Finding ourselves unmoving,
Abundantly concealed by
These great white hours
And all their complex going.

I - 10

IF the soul has no shadow
And our light on earth
Is only moving and transparent,
Making us rise up from
False nameless dark
Suddenly aware and desiring:

As a wind blows careless
Through immaculate distance
In a tall hyacinth sky,
Shaking gold flowers
On a yellow May morning
Affecting how we observe:

Innocent and barely new
Gently exposed in my arms
Beautiful and most assured,
One being of the future and
Two rivers in a life flowing
From ancestral suns and days.

Quick with light, you are
Weightless and so feminine
Daughter of beauty and goodness,
Restoring our good breath
With one just heart-beat
And your optimism.

My delicate sparrow
I am caught in a mesh
Surprised by complete love,
Informed by your promise
Of all possible kindness
Unshaded by guilt or remorse.

~ E R O S ~

Young and perfectible
Veiled bride that you are
Offering us true life:
Accept in your sleep
My grateful ambition
Here - as I take your hand.

I – 11

YOUR gentle sleeping innocence
Whose mild breath inaudible,
Whilst dawn sprinkles rain
Upon lately risen light:

Frugal, fallible, a new world
Before it is to be described,
Defenceless ingenuity of
Unsimulated artless calm.

Undisclosed, without coercion
Your freedom that is unaware,
Where youth and sleep are entire
Context for earth and life.

No one in the world has seen
You so at rest and undisguised,
And as time does not recur
This instant is without record.

Tenderness is a sign perhaps
Of creativity itself,
Imperfect, not repeated
As a future amplifies a past.

Where your womanhood remains
Inhabiting and uncovered,
More of friendship than desire
Yet completely satisfied
Recipient of all balance.

I - 12

As we lay upon a shore
Naked in the smooth hot light,
A blood-warm ocean rolled
Recursively on coral sand.

Stained with phosphoros and kisses
Nuptial powder on our skin,
You made the darkness tuneful
My lioness of silk and tissue.

In the coppery rites of sunset
You were my soul and universe,
In those instants we became
Infinite and changeless.

Before dawn raised its eyes
Exposing so much truth,
From senseless prolific night
As the sun's panels slid apart:

Among the columns of the sea
Its restless frantic tongues,
We were quietly recognised
And our transparency noted.

Time removes all experience
But for a slightest trace,
The strange delays of life and
Its lamps and intervals.

Within a few simple moments
There is treasure folded deep,
And the rest of life is sequence
In the ultra and aquamarine,
There are no errors in love.

I - 13

THE sowing of men and women
Spontaneous, irresistible,
Now in this month of fall
As trees reveal a spectrum
Colours of lost desire.

As with a field and furrow
Where grain is scattered by hand,
We bury the future in darkness
Entering into night.

This knitting together of tissue
Flesh and earth and time,
With you I turn inwards
We close the doors, retire
Our promises on fire.

I - 14

EARTH would show her cities
If asked to reveal herself,
Monuments, embankments
Bridges and all the statues:

A river upon which life
Has flooded and receded,
A brown vein distended
Wealth, trade and flotsam.

Nothing is more fair than
Timeliness of being,
Passion and corruption
Art refining each desire.

A red dawn swells above
Becomes a pure opacity,
Cold air is fine and damp
Vigorous with old life.

Swept away in this flame
Earth relights her loving,
Beauty that is dark and bold
A stone spire of humanity.

The river's mud is bitter
Spawning this essential,
As millennia of ambitions
Run by with their lust.

for Harriet Bridgeman

I - 15

ONTO the zero lake they came
Down from a low nacreous sky,
Their gentle faces soaked with space
With lucid skin and transparent bodies.

Not a living soul was in sight as
They sang of pity for humankind,
Grey drops that fell from their eyes
Were like soft young herons in flight.

As we hurried off along the shore
Seeking minutes somewhere else,
They observed our necessary guilt
And wept for our foolish haste.

In suspense above an emerald lake
Engrained, hovering they wait for us,
For we are their myth and without them
We are untrue, without consequence.

They admire our easy friendship
Feeding us their light wafers,
As their spirit like two snakes
Twines throughout the universe.

Their weightlessness sustains us -
The duration of humanity,
Till one day they repossess
Our strange causeless ways.

I - 16

SOON the swans return and
Shall descend upon the lake,
Gracious, slow, circling down
Towards these cold grey waves.

Signs of life, they are
Touching upon a spring,
With an archery of insight
That strikes recumbent winter.

With so much languid treasure
Gathered by long flight,
These inhabitants of sheer air
Know of life's migration.

They do not give but offer
To those who see their way,
Who silently beside the lake
For years await this presence.

Great white birds who wheel
Gliding down without sound,
As one by one they circle us
Made speechless by their beauty.

Far from a distance they
Bring warmth and consciousness,
So human spirit can abound
In light and kindness and
Being that in time is just.

I - 17

I HAVE seen things in my life
Which no one else has known,
How to say this now, how
To speak of what is vision
For so much is unheard?

I have looked across a river
And seen them there - those
Who have no human name
Whose language has no word,
Faultless with compassion.

As birds of unblemished wing
Perfect with unearthly tone,
They shoot across the candid air
Their shining bodies lucent
Propelled by light and shadow:
Their unfinished songs
Are speechless, full of love
Floating far above our haste.

Beautiful they are and gracious
Luminous within their skin,
As if no worldly life could be
Possessive of such warm body,
A supernatural being walks
Inside their easy going.

Their clear sureness is
Vibrant in a flawless manner,
Generous, gentle, undemanding
Nothing can inhibit them,
In their experience domination
Never can secure a place:
So constantly - I must admire
Observing time in how they play.

I - 18

As a shell that lies upon a lake
Broken into dust and time,
Or mist that dissipates in heat
When white sun warms the ground:

So rain falls upon a river
As a slow current runs away,
And human life evaporates
Leaving but a few drops.

How passion and affection go
Disappear so lightly,
As if there was no love
And no mystery occurred.

Just like an empty shell
Where coldness and cynicism
Lie curled up in a little space,
The moral beauty of the world
Is dissolved by slight darkness.

I - 19

THE small terrors that enclose each day
Genius of time avoiding us,
The art by which we struggle onward
To triumph through such emptiness,
Love with which we build a house.

These are the stones that we arrange
Signs of loneliness and solitude,
When despair removes all sensual life
Enveloped by deep silence
We review the void of living.

Time is ruthless - how it wounds
Our words are broken by the days,
We polish all this desolation
To make a flimsy world accept
A powdery shore and vital place,
There is no love but only vision.

I - 20

THE entirety of human love
Outlaw, impatient, artless,
A seam in which we freely
Choose to run our hand
Joining with the durable.

This is the end, the moment
Origin and conclusiveness,
The surface of duality as
Our only way to correspond:
Our bitterness at fragility and
How the formless crouches
Far within the heart of form.

T W O

THEY come and go and trespass
Freighted with desire,
Young women of the spring
In their summer dresses.

Crocus yellow, hyacinth
Their golden shoulders bare,
A green text burning
Sweet upon their lips.

A mysterious and complex grace
The pleasure of your smile,
The girl in you pretending
That you are not alone.

Be with me beside you now
With the future's breath,
In our sleep we shall resist
And admire the fugitive,
We shall complete the world.

I I - 2

THE nature of my love is this
I witness you as no other,
When you are mine to hold
Refining our warm volume.

I love your bones and your smell
A scent of leaves and rain,
At the hollows of your joints
My hands confess their love.

Asleep with you I have no
Other place on earth to visit,
You are all world and home
Ground where life sets out.

What more is there in time
For us to know, what else
Can human love accomplish,
In you I touch an absolute.

I brush your lips with my tongue
Breathe in your exhaled breath,
Deep inside we perceive
What no one else observes.

I I - 3

LAST night as you lay beside me
The most beautiful of women,
I felt that I was at home
On earth, empowered and mortal.

My concord and my platinum
My peerless assertion,
You - my perfect boundary
My liaison with all of time.

A spray of rain upon the dark
Bloodless obdurate sky,
Outside our room was nowhere
Space lay warm in my arms.

Your legs alongside mine
Our ankles touching casually,
My hand upon your smooth back
As you fell asleep and sighed.

Is there justice in our love
Genius or honesty in life:
Last night I was transfigured
By your immense equilibrium
As I looked upon your smile.

I I - 4

LAST night I held in my arms
The most beautiful thing on earth,
Night of a full May moon
When life once more ascends.

Not joy nor love nor possession
Nor the giving up of passion,
Nor the first lie that made this
Neither regretful nor worldly.

Touched by warm living beauty
Whose curve bent over and rested,
Beside me the sleeping breath
Moved on my lips and face.

Beyond any pattern of minutes
Beyond that invisible wall,
When as a heap of dust we are
Dispersed by a friend or lover:

Last night beauty and goodness
Faultless, fruitless, generous,
Gave itself to my guilty heart
As a window opened on space.

One indestructible night
Further than human expression,
Gentle, stable, desiring to be
Held before it was lost.

I I - 5

TO sleep with you in my arms
Intimate, warm and tender,
Your breath upon my mouth
Your hair upon my shoulder.

Sweetness of your topaz skin
Closeness of your perfect bones,
How you move in the night
As all a world inaudible.

Milky light of low morning
Its citron rays piercing leaves,
Silence of day as animals
Retire to sleep or hide from us.

We who have so very much
Wealth from an original aeon,
Our gold has no currency
But the gestures we exchange.

I I - 6

DO you remember the pink oleander
And the hot breeze of an afternoon,
A courtyard's breathless shade and
Jasmine darkening a night with sweet?

Do you remember the cool of vines
Beneath which we sat and watched,
As bamboo switched in the air and
A turquoise sea crackled and flashed?

How cicadas screeched and rasped
During noon's white ferocity,
Moonlight made a world abstract
Monochrome with silver candour.

Do you recall the lemon blossom
In the square as we walked home
From the port at night, you and I
On that island without a name?

I put some oleander by your bed
Before you woke one morning,
Furtively I watched you sleeping
Flirting beside a watering stream,
In your mind you were not with me.

Where are the paths and groves now
And the heated dust on our skin,
And afternoon behind walls when
We lay down in a shuttered room
Wakening to bathe at a cistern?

I I - 7

THE faint blur that we leave
Upon time and space,
Fragrance of rain at night
A sudden meteor falling.

You, wakening slowly
In your bare white room,
Breaking your illusions
Motionless in sleep.

From far off I watch you
A bird climbing the sky,
Premonitory, quiet, waiting
For you to notice me.

Like light I shall enter
Into your day, your heart,
You will not know that
I have settled inside.

Suddenly you will need me
And I shall be there - but
It all happened long ago
And we are just the trace.

I I - 8

WE shall meet in paradise
You and I, when all this is done,
And the rains have gone and
The wet roads and low dawns,
And winter has crystallised
Become a blue midsummer
An aerial flashing ocean.

Until then let us keep
Nights companionable and
Let us walk together down
More paths than we know,
Keeping close and private
Each furthering the other.

For we shall see in paradise
All the time on earth,
And we shall be like trees
Golden, knowing everything
Our senses like white birds:
Possessing what is unstable
Here in a shifting world,
The circles will be ours and
Each thread of our bodies firm.

I I - 9

WHAT marvel is there more than you
Your golden armour and your guilt,
The gentle snarl provoking love
When I see you in the arms of one
Who has you more complete than I.

But he could never hold you as
In my heart I phrase you now,
In my hands I rule the tongue
Which makes you more than life.

I imitate and I repeat and marvellous
I make you more - more than beauty
More than pleasure, more than warmth
That's his to hold. Central him
But mine to touch with every thought.

I I – 10

My heart is a three-masted boat
A virgin of green and blue seas,
With five sails bent and tugging
And foam splashing from her stem.

You are my ship and voyager
Image of lights charting heaven,
In my heart you were fearless
Then another took you away.

Islands that smell of perfume
Trees that shine in dark hours,
Houses built of sharp white coral
These I thought would be home.

He has you now, tied by a thread
And seas are unbearably calm,
My heart sails alone and bitterly
Dignified, avoiding harbour.

You are still my passage bird
Wheel I hold in my hands,
The soul may dissolve into salt
But the ship is made to go.

I I - 11

WHAT is the incidence of love
When the three stars fly out,
When deception becomes the rule
That is not to be avoided?

Bare trees filter golden dawns
Fretting still molten light,
You are alone without illusion
What can you say to equivocate?

Fugitive yet pointless, turning
About to see a perspective,
Forgetting becomes a creative act
In order to meet with success.

Without the impetus of love
You are a ghost, stalking one,
Everything you mutter aloud
Holds two separated meanings.

What is the instance of love
And those stars, where are they,
Into what sphere do they go
When you hold out your arms?

I I – 12

THOSE who seek perfection in love
And in this are always failing,
Dispossessed, unsatisfied, blackened
By what it is they imagine.

Is it the experience of beauty
Something tangible beyond life,
Or is their vision amoral, unearthly
Leading to this vast displeasure?

Perfectly attuned and tranquil
Caught in silence and dimension,
Discontented by bodies which
Do not calm their immense desire:

Two horses lashed to a wheel
Chasing, circulating darkness,
Escaping only drives them onward
To repeat the same patrol.

I I - 13

ANXIOUS primitive and undesiring
Days fall like yellow leaves,
Under the rain onto the roads
They rush away into oblivion.

How is it that we recall them
And triumph over time's vacuity,
A recollection that reforms us
Makes us alive again, heroic?

Language with its nets and hooks
Pictures with their strange shadow,
Slowly we recapture the creatures
Who ran away one stormy night.

Wandering out there in wild nature
Troubled by their strange solitude,
We entice the days back toward us
To sleep again under one roof.

I I - 14

IN paradise there are no mirrors
For none need to reflect,
Nor are there any memories
Life and days are complete
And nothing is forgotten.

Love has a secret to perfect
Intimate and undisclosed,
The private ring a suitor gives
To one distinguished bride,
Genius informing him
With ideas to accomplish.

'I have no place on earth', he says,
'No kind recollection, only
A strange affiliation for
All that I see before me.

I give myself to you having
No other living wealth,
You are my joyous vision
My rest and every resolution.

Your beaches and your coasts
Islands and fringing hills,
Your pink dawn and setting suns
Air, light, wind, birds - these
I marry to my distance:
For space is all I comprehend
Endless sleepless compulsion.'

I I - 15

AERIAL flowers of evening fall
Indigo powder of night comes,
Uniform, formless and attractive
Compelling and suggestive.

The stiff blue silk of August
Imprinted with courting birds,
Has become limp and colourless
The sky lightless with space.

Summer with its azure eyes
Its green shadows and pools,
Its mercury light filled us
Most happily with illusion.

If we polish the soul daily
A world can be reflected,
Both intimate and abstract
Being constantly bewildered.

Night with all its brightness
Shining and so perfumed,
It satisfies our longing for
The most refined of image -
The invisible heart's clear bell.

I I - 16

WE are like water, you and I
Running through the gorge of time
Unconsumed between white rocks
And smooth bones and black snakes
Where only eagles look down,
Running out toward the sea.

If in many years to come
You return and wander here
I shall be with you in kind
Beneath the arching sunlight,
For you are always in my heart
And I am now like these stones.

As you descend the deep path
In the hot silence of noon,
I shall be watching, hidden
Like the lions on the hills,
For time and beauty were fulfilled
Within our affection.

For there are just two cities
Where a gorge runs between,
I have gone ahead and wait
Where a clear sun never sets:
Where we shall always walk
Among the olive groves through
Long fields towards the ocean.

I I - 17

CICADAS, pigeons, and sound of bells
Suddenly the dawns of long ago
Return fresh and uncluttered,
As if today were simply renewed
And no one had ever gone.

No one had vanished and love
Not lost its promised shape,
No one descended into darkness
Never to walk on earth again
Or look the sun in the eyes and smile.

Life passes but for the plea of children
Voice of women, the prolix sea,
Cicadas telling of just one story
Of how much we possess except
For the consciousness of so much beauty.

I I - 18

My daughter for all her loveliness
In her light-filled weightless way,
Laughs and listens to a music
That no one else perceives.

Her destiny is beyond me yet
She rests in my arms as we
Walk the grounds at night beneath
An ingenuous saffron moon.

Small grains of genius and love
Enter her gentle sanctuary,
Unseen they pause and settle there
Till one day they put out leaves.

This is the secrecy of time
How immortality finds a place,
How it is that truth adheres
Becomes transmitted between souls.

Unaware of the freight we bear
Its indifference and monotony,
Our reckless life and impatience
Reveal an easy timelessness.

We do not know what we convey
Of universal privacy,
Forms of beauty and of music
Like the unison of love itself
Are prescient with sunlight.

I I - 19

SHE appears in the world as if
From an envelope of the same,
And as a girl she is composed
By small gestures of affection.

In youth she learns to imitate
Before she learns to pretend,
Dazzled by masculinity she
Offers herself as its place.

Only once in her life is a woman
Given by hand in marriage,
And then she lightly appears
Supernatural in her beauty.

As a wife loving provides her
With a vision of potential,
How it is to move in time
Without being distracted.

Then with her children she
Assumes more than she knows,
Giving more than she possesses
She is mutual with the world.

She grows pliable as her family
Acquire their own desires,
A matron - she revives pleasure
Acting without converse.

At last as a widow she is
Generous, easy with laughter,
For betrayal and ordeal have
Exposed the nature of virtue
And the power of her words.

I I - 20

As the sun enters the lion
Chromium dust filters evening,
Time becomes like a dim water
Where we go without saying
Upon a glittering reflective sea.

The nerveless unconscious ocean
Where life thinks of nothing,
Disembodied and pleasurable
Lust is simply visible
And there is no efficacy:

Where the soul leaves a body
Mourning the memory it deserts,
Naked, without desire as
It hurtles through night and space
Towards unimaginable islands.

Where the sun never settles
And there are only white birds:
Lion of human luminosity
Going lightly among the hours
Beneath the eyelids of long day.

I I - 21

A REARING lion like a magnet
Draws the soul into itself,
Years gather slowly round
Touch their forehead to the earth.

Once there was a life that tried
To clarify the names and words,
In its vision of a world
To triumph with a simple point.

Brazen light of morning sweeps
The globe like a dancing place,
A flat bright disc upon which
Creatures meet to kiss and part.

Leopards rise up and sing now
Panthers at night are monotone,
Eagles bend their necks down
Both in praise and mourning.

Love will take us on and straight
From struggle or what we destroy,
Love that never shudders when
Dissolved by a voice in the fire.

Hope was a hull made of leaves
Belief the bubble in its compass,
Transmitted, it told its story
Suspended between waves.

The lions disappear at once
Their image hovering on the air,
Invisible beauty gathers close
Waiting for the next call
When humanity cries out.

for Philip Sherrard

I I - 22

TO emulate the cry of love
Its carnal wish inborn to life,
What is it we should say
That knows of no reply?

With daring or with cynicism
Which blows through space
Moving being: act, effect
Or condition, every call.

So many cattle of the soul
Driven from a potter's wheel
Onto a sea of burning white
Raise their heads to speak.

What will free us, undo silence
Catching us upon its round,
Is there a love that will loosen
Pleasure that will go beyond?

My god, the terror of this place
Is there nothing we can say,
Extinguished like a match
We are, not to be repeated.

I I - 23

WHEN every passion vanishes
Adhesive to the human heart,
No longer prey a soul
Is dustless and undying.

The hawk of spirit rising
Like fire it enters light,
An impulse purely heat
As the food of time.

Fearless and intangible
Folded throughout space,
The soul assumes the traveller
Who meeting any creature
Equals the desire to play.

I I - 24

WHERE is the boat, I do not see it
The banded moon is already there,
Did you weep, stepping aboard
Was the passage complicated?

Are there lemon trees growing
And white birds among the bells,
Do you feel refreshed and strong
Having shed your old worn skin?

The orange blossom must smell sweet
Erotic, thanatic, the leaves pungent,
How is it when there is always light
Sunless, sleepless, without change?

Perhaps they were the oars I heard
Slow locks squeaking and dripping,
As I woke before dawn yesterday
And your house was all closed up.

for Gordon Miln

I I - 25

THE saffron fragrance of the ocean
The effulgence of its space,
The undyed depths whose origins
Like memory are not to be discerned
Where all lives remain unknown.

The red sails of antiquity
Aeons of quiet suffering,
And our joy when the sea
Procreates endlessly for us,
Milky waves forever breaking.

The sea seduces us with
A pitiless complete beauty,
Without demands, without gifts
Without content and unconstrained
Offering to us its own image:
A perfume that exceeds all
We might ever know on earth.

I I - 26

BOATS are coming out of the light
Into the roar of human suffering,
Yet here and there points of love
Shine and sparkle lucidly.

There are no surprises any more
Nothing to redeem our ways,
A plenitude of struggle and hope
Leaves us alone on a vacant shore.

It is not that time passes us by
But we who recede from time,
Constant and immutable it
Leaves us only glancing.

Then it is not love we see
But strange ghosts who are made
In our image as we grow quiet,
No one knows why we do as we must.

There is so much beauty on earth
Transporting us out of our lives,
Yet when the boats come to take
Our thin bare souls away
Beauty is silent and only withdraws.

I I - 27

BOOMING down towards Kythera
With five sails bent and tugging,
A white hull through the waves
Breaking ultra and aquamarine.

With you beside me at the wheel
And all of life behind us,
The island on our starboard bow
Within a coruscating distance.

The apex of our known world
Quivering on the horizon,
Amorous together – you and I
Among the groves and saplings.

Our anchor firm within a bay
Riding out the warm nights,
A ruined citadel upon the cliffs
Outlined by constellation.

What is the extent of time
With which we are provided,
As I hold you in my arms
The vessel rocking in the dark?

How to make the voyage last
Beyond anything we know,
What words are possible now
That can take us further?

Beyond Kythera towards where
Our boat will sail herself,
Out of time's circumspection
Fluctuating in the light
Where our fame will always go.

I I - 28

HOURS on the ship, timbers creaking
As the boat swayed and lunged
Into a damp marine night running,
The vessel remorseless, unthinking
Engines beating like blood,
Sails rattling and cracking as
The mast-head dipped like a stylus
Among pure white inky stars.

Hours on the ship with you
Down in our wooden cabin,
Falling asleep beside you
Our bodies wet with love:
In a saffron dawn that streamed
Through a small porthole,
You moved closer against me as
I inhaled your sweet warm breath.

Hours on the ship as if
There was no land nor earth
We became strangely infinite:
The flying-fish and the flags
The bells and circling weather,
As night after night below
Folded into our quiet selves
We rose and fell oblivious
Intimate with an ancient ocean.

I I - 29

As the soul flutters away from its ashes
Insensible, helpless, powerless,
Purified of this doubtful life
By being washed with cleansing fire,
Is there any single thread attaching
Us to a lightless ungraven being
Or are we translated repeatedly?

Old shipmate, companion, voyager
Where are we bound on this ocean,
As the boat sinks away from sight
Into a grey-green and bluish deep
And the last smoke rises from shore:
Towards what new life are we destined
Naked without women or shadow?

The heroes have wandered far away
Gone in search of those whom only
They were able to call and love:
An unburnt dust of remaining friends
Hovers about a rough damp pit,
Keen and thirsty to drink of blood
Released from the cycle of truth.

We are free of bodies for just a while
Before we suffer these worlds again,
Perpetually changing upon a coast
Between sea, life, and desiring death
Necessity was the wheel of our passion,
As soul arises to frequent the air
To annul our further migration.

Nature draws us with implication
Strips us and leaves us under the sun,
On a pebbled beach where like lovers
We enjoy the heat of a shimmering day:
As cicadas rave inland on rocks
And lust bleaches our souls dry
Discharging the ancient guilt.

All things come at last to a chasm
Where carnal justice cannot exist:
Solemn unclothed affection of youth
Bare immemorial pathways
All forgetfully ruined,
As we leave behind the universe
Entering a pure black void of nil.

Old mariner, pilot, captain of time
Seven seas and a white vessel await,
Shake out the canvas and throw off
Those anchors and useless oars:
Let us embrace the horizon and go
Beyond the ultimate fire of zenith,
Where none will recognise our spirit
And soul like a quick white bird is gone.

for Richard Warren Vick

I I - 30

UNDER the olive trees of old youth
We loved and slept and imagined,
As along the coasts and on
Stony sunlit hills we wandered.

The necessity of imperfection
In all our breathing life,
In the slow struggles we engage
In order to arrive somewhere.

We forget and abandon days
When hours were limitless,
In a continuous fading of beauty
Becoming continual darkness.

There is blackness to be endured
If we are to reach eminence -
An oblivion of human emptiness
Until that vivid light returns.

Suddenly those dancing trees
Appear and surround our days,
And upon that earth and shadow
We once more rest a while
As time leaves us alone again.

I I - 31

ALL those who in life have gone
To the shore of the sea of being,
An ocean of potential where
They forever patrol the coast
Awaiting further commands:

A molten sky and shadowless ground
Turbulence of invisible waves,
A grey-blue unoriginal light
Where life takes its primary pulse,
The quiet roar of everything.

All the nights in one's life do not
Always end with the dawn,
Sometimes we find ourselves
On the margins of an absolute sea,
Where a sun can neither rise
Nor set and only souls dwell.

I I - 32

HOW all of experience only
Deceives us with its air,
Glistening impermanence
Duplicity of two worlds.

We live as in a gateway
Like a watchman sleeping,
As past and future travel
In and out of a city.

Into our open mouths
So much water is pouring,
Never to be consumed
Nor to allay our thirst.

How wonderful is time
Gorgeous like a kingfisher,
Quick, brilliant and gone
Before we glance twice.

In solitude we struggle
With giants and armies,
Shadows we perceive
Consider to be true.

If the sun has a memory
Let it now awaken us,
You and I pretending
We are going nowhere
And the city absolute.

I I - 33

LIKE giants bowed in anxious thought
My memories of you sit about me now,
Weighing my shoulders and oppressing
All attempt to recall your presence.

Sometimes they moan and move around
And in my sleep you return to me,
Wakening, there remains no trace
Just the same grey motionless figures.

If we are a glass which holds the dust
Measuring out our time on earth,
Sometimes the giants turn us and
We can reclaim some of our laughter.

So many grains of memory
Crowding into a single room
Ponderous, unquiet in their oblivion,
Unconscious, solitary shapes who
Are unaware of you and me.

I I - 34

THE immortals are all about us
Yet they do not know their names,
Sometimes it is their suffering
Their loneliness and remorse
That releases them from being
The desperation of this place.

Then they perform their worth
Their music and their words,
With vision and compassion, love
Pacifying and conceiving for
We who live and walk the earth
Remain obscured by flames.

Their genius and lightness go
Sovereign and easily,
The quietness and softness of
Their joy is for us so firm,
Beautiful and kindly as
They reflect their force upon us.

Inscrutable and undestined
Enduring darkness in the world,
Their despair for an earthly void
Illuminates our hesitation
With signs of slowest passion:
Then one day they are gone and
We recall them in human prayer.

I I - 35

IT is not what we leave
But what we go towards
That counts in the end:
For nothing is ever still
There is no unmoving,
In each other's eyes
We only breathe and dwell.

Accomplishment is nil
If it does not send us on
Towards what we do not
Know or cannot gain:
For nothing is ever lost
In our recollection.

T H R E E

NOT just a single beauty
But all the passing states
The various and manifest,
Each day another form:

Once in flamingo
Another time a heron,
Soaring through the quick light
Or as a sparrow laughing:

Her beauty was ephemeral
Never once paused,
So many women were
In her body as she walked.

Blue as a kingfisher
Who shot out her glances
With so much rapid grace,
Then each day she vanished.

When I held her in my arms
She changed before my eyes,
Lucid and transforming as
She was not here on earth.

How I loved this woman
Who was always receding,
Drawing me away from
The time that I knew well.

One morning I awoke
As she lay beside me,
And then at last I saw
Her beauty deep inside
As all the world approached.

III - 2

IN a soft blue cyanine light
As I walked out one afternoon,
Herds were passing beneath trees
The land hovered in dust and heat.

I walked for miles the powdery ways
A few hawks swooped to see me,
And then returned across the earth
Between thorn and dry hedges.

Upstairs in a cool dark room
Shutters locked against the sun,
You were resting with eyes closed
And stripping, I lay beside you:

Finding perfection in your arms
Your slowness like rain,
As you lightly rest asleep
With my hands I adore you.

I walked among the trees at night
Singing of my admiration,
As beneath the perfect sky
You and I strolled at dusk.

The threads of our desiring
Tangle and knot themselves,
I am fixed by your beauty
Your simple easy form.

As owls in the fruit trees
And peacocks in the deep grass
Warily observe your calm
And listen to my words telling:

So I am bound and tied up
By loving you and keeping
Beside you as we cross these fields,
Yet there is no real going.

For how is it I cannot
See myself and yet perceive you,
And in my eyes at night
Your beauty is my world?

Shadows gather in the leaves
As we pass through the orchard,
Small snakes avoid our footfall
As silence gathers round.

Wind moving in the foliage
Like rainfall sounds on pebbles,
My voice, your breath, the air
All these mix and this is pleasure.

Sleep – and I shall always sing
As I look upon your features,
You are more than I have known
All affection and surrender.

As light reaches nadir or
A bird vanishing in space,
So my passion counters you
As it introspects your days.

Like a reflex concealed
Or the fruit of being human,
As you rest in my arms untroubled
I shall be your instrument
As we cross the enduring earth.

For the witnessing of love is
An unbearable perfection,
Fugitive and nameless it
Pauses in no one place:
Always to be seen through
Love cannot be exchanged.

Quietly and most freely
It cannot be withheld,
Truly viewed through silence
It never keeps to just one way:
There is no end to love
Its beauty does not change.

I I I - 3

As we looked out from a hilltop
One waterless blazing afternoon,
Some starved pigeons launched themselves
Into voluminous space to be
Driven back by a forceful wind.

Time like a cruel bird enters
Penetrates the tentative world,
Feeding on optimism and compassion
Experience is superceded
There is no possible recollection.

Perhaps like the rings of a tree
Happiness and the experience of truth
Are impressed upon our fragile hearts,
Moments are unremembered
And we retain no recollection:

Like shadows passing on the sea
Convex in a humid air,
Where quiet fishermen cast their nets
And solemnly await a sign as
Art, vision, love, dissolve.

So we walked back to the plain
Into a tawny evening where
We are worn away by hours and
Youthfulness is exchanged for night
In twilight like a coral mineral.

There is no translation possible
In the cadence and spray of years,
A moist surface of ash or dust
Or the oily stain of smoke only
Adheres to a blackened instrument.

Confronted by intangible light
We cannot sustain one single ideal,
No one aspect of life is conveyed
Whatever the unrelenting migration:
As it slowly crosses another plateau
The spirit only arrives at itself.

That afternoon as we walked the hills
A herd of deer circled about us,
Their movement given away by an egret
A white point moving on air.

Those gently mounded magenta hills
Where seashells and agates lay scattered,
Like an ancient broken reef of rock
That reared up from the plain and fields:

A lark was singing above the summit
Rising and vanishing into the sky,
As you and I lay on the stones
Discussing love and vicissitude.

'There is neither attachment nor meaning,'
You said, 'Which only leads to sorrow:
Where is belief or great joy,
Is there nothing we can keep with us?'

The herd carefully watched from a distance
The lark climbed higher and vanished,
Below us the land for miles extended
Lost in haze and unspoken years.

'There is amity and companionship
A sharing of days as we walk and pause,
Illuminated not dispossessed - we
Are freed of illusion that wrecks love:

So let us not lose ourselves,' I said,
'Stay true to our one good fortune.'
We descended later that afternoon
Having accomplished more than we knew,
In gathering moments closely about us
Thin blue shadows circled the earth.

I I I - 4

As I walked the evening fields
In a low apricot light,
Cattle were returning slowly
Birds passed the horizon.

A lapwing rose and cried aloud
For suffering and for sorrow,
As sudden kingfishers declared
Contempt for the world's grief.

A hawk lay dead upon the grass
Eaten by flies and ants,
There is victory in decay
In the origin of our joy.

Drums were sounded in the twilight
As bells clashed with songs,
In a humid sultry air
Desolation called its name.

So much beauty on the earth
So much human solitude,
An emptiness of remorse
Confronted by perfection.

In disuse is found our source
In ruin lies the spirit,
As I crossed the dusty fields
Nothing more was to be said,
There is sleep and oblivion.

As I set out that afternoon
To walk the subdued land,
Herds were ambling homeward
And the sky was low and dense.

I wept for the landscape as
A scattering of rain passed by,
For the dying trees and starving fields
For the thin hungry light.

Birds sang in the subtle air
Regardless of anguish,
A snake hunted in a ditch
Careless of the falling world.

If the soul is indestructible
There is no possible sorrow,
There is irony in our desire
And sadness at so much loss.

I soon returned that evening
Pretending that this was true,
That sorrow must be deathless
And loneliness not destroyed
Despite our quiet loving.

Like a dyer's hand submerged
Imbued by submission,
The heart is patterned by experience
Receiving its impression as
It struggles free of condition.

Yet it remains apart from all
That rests upon this tissue,
Coloured and imprinted by
The mordant hand of time
With repetitious seasons -
The transparent genius of all
The hours and weightless life.

For the human soul does not travel
Except to lose its envelope,
Desperate to discard sensation
And embrace the master light.

That supra-light calls out
For a perfect witness to perceive,
Saying, 'I am the zero and
The one who makes things meet.

I am looking for a child
Both vulnerable and weak,
Who has the patience to pursue
The sole fiction of truth:

The cities of the future
Seen only in a vision,
When human sight turns inward
And moves away from time.

For spirit like a thread
Encircles what it needs,
Tightening and loosing lives
Like a silhouette it goes.

Assembled in their chains
Entering each others' bodies,
How far do the living step
Furthering what they receive?

There is an arrow to this life
See – the bloody missile moving,
As darts and javelins of love
Touch upon humanity:

Consuming all achievement
And devouring ambition,
Breaking the ideal membrane
The sensual and conceptual.'

Pale-blue, alkaline, ephemeral
Invisible, the master light,
Traceless on the vivid earth
Withdrawing from existence,
Poignant with despond, weeping
Leaving us to walk alone.

I I I - 5

As we sat upon a hill-top
Amazing at its vision,
Flat land for miles receded
Between ocean and plateau.

So much time lay beneath us
Sheathed in lucid space,
Years and their endeavour
Their doubt and anxiety.

Now we were justly balanced
As beneath us flocks and herds
Quietly roamed the terrain
With no place on earth.

Prophecy and its glare
Fell away from those hours,
Above the distant glassy lakes
And that gentle frugal ground.

A hare bolted from a bush
A merlin hovered in suspense,
Beneath our feet were crimson stones
And here and there lay agates.

How the soul is chained to time
And the guilt of experience,
As beneath a quartz sky
We wandered with our vanity.

An iron summer dust was
Sleeping on the printless ground,
With its purple minerals and
The glitter of a faithless world.

From that pausing afternoon
There was nothing elusive,
Transfigured by the warm light
We stood above the turning plain.

Silence and patience drew us
To that lonely focal spot,
From one great periphery
We had circled for a life.

Upon the body of the year
The texture of a soul is traced,
Repeatedly our hearts are
Made perfect by that reflex.

It was as if our footsteps
Were expunged from that point,
And from that moment onwards
We could walk without fault.

Granted life by the distance
Viewed apart from time,
Beneath us the vision moved
With a semblance of unknowing
From the black hills to the ocean.

III - 6

As we walked out one evening
Leaving tracks upon the sand,
Our steps were soon overlaid
With marks of foxes and of birds.

It is genius which makes us see
Offering us a vision where
We observe those ancient beings
Who barely watch our passing ways.

They honour us with their feet
As they cross the blank-white earth,
Gathering at the frontiers
Where humanity stands at a threshold.

Quail and partridge rise at dusk
As drums and bells are sounded,
The universe reveals its fire
With soft flame and vermilion smoke.

Nothing stays but this emotion
Of one pure afternoon in space,
As all the lives gathered round
Witnessing our independence
When love sat before us.

So in time's genius is
This hidden source of pleasure,
Of stability and harmony
Of vicissitude, and there
The sovereign light combines
All lives within one wheel,
And that is our secret frame:

Which few unlock and fewer
Are able to perceive its walls,
Only a clear spirit moves
Freely in and out those rooms,
Like birds whose mutual exchange
Consists of songs and migration
Beyond the present and its ranging.

The year turns on its hinges
With glittering days of sheer
Glassy labile sensuous heat,
Giving way to milky zones
Of cool and shining moisture:
As hills renew their life
Sleepless birds sing aloud
Excited by this novel green.

In whose cells and potent combs
Birds mourn a former joy,
For the fiery seclusion
They once loved to observe,
When their flying souls were true
In the first express of flight:

As we walked out one evening
The land was still at rest,
Birds cried and fields were sombre
No humanity was working.

We crossed the empty distance
Pausing beneath quiet trees,
Whose soft reserve satisfied
Our eyes from the sun's glare.

Who knows where we are going
For time has no one point,
We continue and we forget
So much suffering and joy.

Genius rises from attachment
Speaking from beyond itself,
Moving further than a life
Its words possess no single body.

As we walked out that evening
Covered by obscurity
There was a fluttering in the air
As if the stars were being loosed:

Then soul exposed its only place
Going on the ancient dust,
Admiring earth's first columns
Among the meteors and pebbles.

III-7

IN a low grey luminous light
Along the coast in shining air,
When the tide retreated leaving
Sands glistening and bare for miles,
Some flamingoes passed overhead.

They curved about and turned away
Undistracted in their intent,
Gracious with a slow movement
Perfect in formation and tempo
As they winged the lucid emptiness.

Their delicate quiet silence
Sublime with disregard,
As the ocean turned and folded
Breaking open and retreating,
The birds passed on and disappeared.

One pure spot of dazzling colour
Upon a monochrome evening,
Loveliness and equanimity joined
Avoiding human experience,
In their solitary unmarked way
Untroubled by our presence.

Along the shore and whitening sky
As a tide broke heavy and disordered,
The sands reflected a blue heaven
Filmed by a receding ocean.

Standing apart in isolation
Far from life or any movement,
A crowd of tall serene flamingoes
Browsed upon shimmering pools.

Brilliant in their pink apparel
As if pausing from another world,
Exquisite in their unconcern
Careless of human loneliness.

Suddenly rising to the air
In long and gracious strokes,
They glided off down the wind
Seaward and disappeared.

Such beauty is not for this time
Unearthly and super-natural,
The flamingoes vanished from our sight
Too strangely perfect to remain
Upon this desolate vacant coast.

I I I - 8

AMONG the pillars of the world
Hidden behind obvious displays,
The guardians of our lives reside
Awaiting accomplishment and love.

It is the fragrance of emptiness
That makes us see ourselves,
A loneliness that aches always
Craving recognition in time.

This living presence of duration
Where a heart's disquiet finds calm,
Above the mountain birds pause
Hanging on the wind's fluency:

Solitude and independence
The mystery of our being,
Impersonation of frail days
And taming of impatience.

Above the plain there is a fire
Burning openly in space,
Emitting heat that gives time force
And blood that makes love wet.

Streaming with this liberal passion
The fire dies and then returns,
Copulating with itself, the flames
Are made of jackals and of leopards.

From the summit looking out
Our lives appear in apparition,
Human efficacy is discarded
As we walk the earth and disappear
When the guardians call our names:

Where time has no recess
And sinuous minutes provide
No nourishing grain to thrive
Beneath this acrid dome of life.

If days are a singular effort
To capture the fugitive
Experience or the emotions that
Expire like birds from sight:

How shall we ever possess
Love, beauty, or vision,
Accomplishing what is certain
Composing a brief memory?

So much is received and yet
So little stays in hand,
As joy and even sorrow recede
Lost to the invisible light,
No harvest is observed.

Once when the earth was slow
We walked openly and unconfined,
Sun and moon would show their beauty
Keeping us within their bounds.

Then we were strong with easiness
Saw men and women of the world
Going as if they simply possessed
Time with festival content.

Fields reproduced and dried themselves
Trees laid down their moist leaves,
Tedious cattle and herds went out
As coloured birds appeared and vanished.

There is a place where we can walk
Where paths are obvious and land
Is warm at night and fearless as
Water comes down from the stars.

If we do not pursue those ways and
Keep to the noise of human cities,
We shall never know the breath of shadow
Beneath love's embroidered cloth
A gentleness that breaks suffering.

For solitude has no place
There is no light to solitude,
True solitude is without person
Alone without name or body,
So versatile and sensitive it
Cannot discern one thing.

Solitude does not forget
For it has no memory,
It merely presents the world
Always remaining silent.

It is the keeper of our soul
Compassionate, unspeaking,
Watching for our indiscretion
When we forget ourselves.

I I I - 9

ON my fifty-fifth year on earth
I walked out at Pragsar,
Beside the lake and crimson hills
To observe the many birds.

It had been lightly raining
The land was transient green,
The sky unusually sapphire
With a border of white.

Flocks of young grey herons
Dashed across the air,
As pairs of kingfishers paused
Above the celadon water.

I thought of the sea and coasts
So present in my youth,
As we gently crossed that plain
In order to look out.

For this day the first sails
Had appeared far at sea,
Small brown triangles bending
Low upon the horizon.

As we approached the high rocks
A panther with her cubs,
Gently slipped away as if
She did not need to exist.

This had once been panther country
Long ago in the clear past,
Now there was pure silence
And a sweetness to the air.

At a shrine upon the plain
A man and woman prayed,
Pouring milk upon a stone
As they offered up their bodies.

So much in life disappears
As does time itself,
And we are left gazing
Inwardly, away from the world.

Sea, panther, time, stone
Conflate as they retreat,
As if we are without efficacy
And nothing remains of the soul.

Perhaps it is an envelope
Which we merely inhabit,
Maintaining us with sensation
Making us sensitive.

Staring out over Pragsar
Trying to discern the future,
A tide was about to turn
Towards a nameless ocean.

My wife, sons, central art
Long years of slowly walking,
How the soul migrates through time
Yet is completely unknowing.

Now this terrain inhabits me
Its earth is in my heart,
Its unseen beneficence
Brings me to rest.

Tall storks drifted overhead
Desultory kites glided,
Cranes on extended wings
Circled down toward the water.

Like birds going on the air
We leave no sensible trace,
Oscillating heaven and earth
The causes are beyond us.

On my fifty-fifth year of breathing
As we stood upon that hill,
Love showed me its possession
And whispered of its proof,
The secrets of adherence
And the knowledge it assumes.

I I I - 10

I LOVE to watch your beauty
Naked in its lovely form,
Refined, sophisticated, graceful
Like a bird gliding easily
Above wet and reflective sands.

Swimming with you in the sea
As it rises and falls and breaks,
Upon this brown and deserted shore
As a heavy wind fills the air
Noisily sweeping through space.

A sea of silvery-mettle energy
Relentless and always ungiving,
Turbulent and demanding of life
Empty, bare, and inhuman
Interior and carnal.

Joined in time, we are
As if come from millennia,
Made free from all those years
Exchanging destiny and company,
Two bodies simply matched.

To love and to admire the days
Where we walk together,
Sometimes submerging in the waves
As they unfold on this rare coast,
Where you and I find ourselves
Glistening and shining with love.

Yet there is a ship of hours
Circulating in the shadow,
Source of the transparency
Discretion and asymmetry
Of desire within our hearts.

Creating us to be alone
Always to pursue another,
The origin of metaphor
Within the world and why
We are displaced on earth.

The ship arrives and rests
Its worn sails hanging loosely
To dry in the passing wind,
As the boat heels and inclines
Its hull upon the tidal sands
Glad the journey is complete.

What is this impulse we possess
To see the world continuously,
Pursuing those ephemeral signs
All the visible phenomena
Descended from overt forms,
Is there omniscience to this?

We depart and walk the decks
Upon a sea without life,
Air, stars, the endless motion
Of sterile, brackish undulation
Where even birds are silent
And there is nothing to be recalled.

Let us guide the vessel now
Towards another shore and trees,
Where time will find its balance
And supernal release.

For ships arise and then they fade
Like years they come and go,
Upon the sand keels are laid
Trees are felled and prepared,
Old canvas gathers in the wind
A current takes the boats away.

Midsummer – here in this hot land -
We once again visit the sea,
Tumultuous and breaking upon
A coast unchanged in centuries.

Whilst far off in a hazy light
Ships are waiting on anchor,
Unearthly and without any life
They appear apart from time.

It is as if our mundane mystery
Had become so faultless,
As subtle air and ocean fuse
Spilling us onto that shore.

There is eloquence to unknowing
An effortless combination of
Two lives in luminous creation
Bearing a single small child.

Have you seen the slight impression
Upon a pillow at evening,
A sentient damp fragrance
That a soul leaves upon rising?

Here on midsummer afternoon
We return to this coastline,
To bathe in the adamant waves
Whilst our shadows inhabit another land.

As mind wanders among words
And the spirit visits life,
A traveller goes about the world
Until freed from all conditions
The visceral ribbon of kind.

I I I - 11

A CURTAIN is drawn downward
And eyelids gently close,
Memory is overdrawn and sleep
Quietens a restless brain.

Time has disappeared for us
The palace become an ideal,
Upon the lake night descends
As brown water recedes.

Statues fall, sand is blown
Yet human dignity and kindness
Although they cannot incise stone
Etch the world ineradicably.

A sun settles to a tawny desert
As within a shadowed courtyard
Dogs and children play noisily -
Cries and voices that never fade.

So an age turns into light
Another language is exchanged,
Humanity forgets its promise
The old order is unheard.

Humility once ruled this land
Its goodness without effort,
Where rising up with the dawn
Consciousness was amazed that
Life should wear such beauty.

I I I - 12

THE voice of a falcon calls me away
To put aside all human effort,
To leave this world alone and
Go out of time across the sands.

There is no solitude on earth
That is our transparent mystery,
If we are strong enough to give
Our love in exchange for vision.

Who dares to surrender and
Walk barefoot among the stars,
Who will sleep with dust and stone
Taking pleasure in the coldness?

There is no one life we can know
Where we might exceed ourselves,
Untiring in the pursuit of
Being that does not exist.

The rasping whistle of a raptor
As it skims above the trees,
Vacancy and loneliness await
In the voice of that bird,
Beauty proclaiming its only name.

I I I - 13

THERE is a little painted boat
With a stone man for its crew,
It never settles to any shore
And its cargo is the soul of life.

In a frantic and undying wind
We stare at the sun a while,
Then as the boat approaches we
Exchange our world for water.

Friendship with its sharp fragrance
Among the orchard trees
Supplied us with a source of time,
We loved and dwelled and reproduced.

As the worthless painted boat appeared
To retrieve us from life,
It was kindness given by the sun
That allowed us to meet on earth
And to pause for a while.

III - 14

THE outward movement of a soul
Passing throughout space,
Ideal in its affinity
With grammar and perspective
Of human contemplation.

On a constant sea of effort
Where an empty boat sails,
Caught upon a saline flood
Currency of affection and
Medium of our being:

A king and queen are standing
Without earthly commotion
Poised and indifferent,
Unspeakable and beautiful
Is their friendship with this land.

Moving outward from their feet
Are the ways they have walked,
Guarding the moral hours
The old tissue of human lore
Made perfect by devotion.

This is an arrow we do not see
Passing the surface of days,
We observe its moving shadow
Tense of its sharpness and
Oblivion the missile conveys.

What is creativity
Or genesis of true love,
Language spoken before time
Before the speech of birds
Before light was distinct?

The bareness of our solitude
Emptiness of volition,
Quietness of being alone
Companionless and undone
Without emotion or thirst:

We are transmitted by life
Beginning from perfection,
By the magnitude of this vision
Without breathing or
The virtue of duration.

A sparse new rain is falling
Softening the old dust,
Small weak shadows gather
Beneath the strong rough stone,
The wind bears another life:

A suave acumen of light
Sharp, watery, and still,
As the season loses itself
Falling down to dark space
Of limitless diurnal ocean.

Sometimes the king and queen
Walk the days unobserved,
Their joy and suffering unseen
Before they vanish from the world,
As if this body had no bearing
Was suddenly effaced.

How to speak their names and
Make the universe effective,
To touch the hand of those
Who elected to be patient and
Who made time true for us
Upon this weightless surface?

for Pragmulji

I I I - 15

INDIFFERENT are the runners
Those foretellers of time,
Who, sleeping on the cold earth
Await red morning light.

As they crouch about a fire
Whose small flames of thornwood
Reach into black air,
One or two quietly sing:

'Inanimate the sky and
Immanent the universe
Yet inevitable our end,
Soon we are all invisible and
Creativity and affection
Will never have even moved.'

FOUR

HERE ON this nutmeg island
Lovely as a wreck of paradise,
Where the gentle squalls pass
Lightly overhead and sprinkle
The ground with a moist spray:

A vibrant windward ocean
Sends its breezes shoreward,
To humming-birds and grackles
Who chatter all the day as
Sweet rainbows come and go.

Here where balm of darkness
Black indigo of inky quiet
Is tuned by frogs and insects
And foam sifting on the reef,
Waves unfold - breaking open.

Where admirals are all dead
And the captains deceased,
The great ships disappeared
And stone walls collapsed,
Iron become a green rust.

Here on this volcanic isle
Of clove trees and pepper,
Where vast oceanic swells
Rebound and flow backward
From bare sandy littorals:

Where frigate-birds are soaring
And women carry broad knives,
The men dive for shells and
Sometimes hunt small whales
From narrow-rigged canoes.

Here, where liquid fireflies
Splash their yellow fluid,
Bursting softly and vibrating
Like orange drops of flame,
Nocturnal and gleaming.

Here in fragrant darkness
As ocean booms and shudders,
Flexing in its currents and
Shifting listless vagrant moods,
Unimpassioned, unrelaxing:

Here human consciousness
Is ever static and unmoving,
As all a world scintillates
Rich in unseen potence like
Sulphur orchids in the mountains.

All is patience here and tincture
Nothing ever is distinct,
Merging, humid, unaffected
Like owls and mosquitoes -
Unobserved, invisible.

At night ships ride on anchor
Hovering on a viscid swell
Near the susurrating reef,
Their lights glow like suave eyes
As if existence were not full.

Sometimes the air implodes
Soundless in the rhythmic night,
On an empty blissful sea
Where storms flourish in suspense
Alone from terrestrial life.

Monsoon oleander skies
Hours of slow terrific rain,
An intense blood-heat dampness
Creates a redolent corrosion -
Light cracks and sparkles sharply.

It is the ephemeral that makes
Life beautiful in this place,
That we might bear witness
And time not be futile so
We can possess a little more.

Here the days are vast and pure
The surf tinged electrically,
Startling and covert white
As clouds like giant beings skim
Somnolent, benign and tedious.

Here where aging sailing ships
Fix their moorings to the coral,
Where languid ospreys float
And palm trees are decaying
As shipwrecks sway innumerable.

Here where dead sailors sleep
Beneath smooth mildewed stones,
In their calm blank sea-graves
Beneath plantains and acacia
Where the termites make their home:

Where the naked shipwrights build
Their new and polished vessels,
Bending planks and caulking hulls
Cutting their strong ribs whole,
As wives stitch prayers and sails.

Sea-wives with green vivid eyes
And blond-almond tattooed skin,
Perfumed with oil of grenadine
Wearing coloured asian cotton
With thick crude iron bracelets.

Where flaws of a caressing wind
Are superficial to the touch,
For the sea does not respond
And fish are oblivious to
Hurricanes that swing about.

In this ginger tamarind land
Of lizard and of anaconda,
Smoke moves slack and negligent
Like uncoiling time itself
To contract and expand at will.

Only a present obtains here
Without reference or migration,
The feminine leaves no trace
And the male holds no power
Nor claim to genealogy.

The fragile vigour of the air
A coruscating sheer horizon,
Where a scented placid landscape
With indolent fertility
Cloys senseless frangipani noon.

Where life is prolific and
No thing becomes redundant,
Birds are like a flickering
Of vital sentient ideas and
Constellations are unobserved.

Here the women meet their men
In a low pink leafy dusk,
As their sweat drips like milk
With odours of lime and rum
They fall asleep exhausted.

Where youths pray each twilight
To the supernatural forces
Who live on hills and peaks,
And girls wash in the morning
Importunate of conception.

Their lust is like a sap or juice
Like a sea rich with crustacea,
Or waves throwing out detritus
Or mahogany trees on fire
Torn with the weight of fruit.

Where the centipedes and ants
Live in ease and desuetude,
A gibbous moon their deity as
Among the flamboyant trees
They live and die unaware:

Where cisterns and slimy wells
Send out small bats at dusk,
Whose private mental lamps
Let them brush against the hair
Of those who walk in solitude:

In the woodland of macaws
Swift noisy parakeets
Dash and flit and brashly scream,
As they play on fecund vines
And small brown snakes are quiet.

Our ankles in a warm sea-foam
As we walk among the ruins,
All a world becomes unlived
Rapacious without motion
On this shining candid coast:

An immense marine amplitude
With its ancient bleached jetsam,
Where barracuda run and leap
Like spikes of darting metal -
A mirror-glass of instant flight.

The brief barracuda songs
Of violence and destruction:
Annihilation of their hero
Who died beyond the reef
Sinking away unlit, unknown.

Herons, egrets, kingfishers
Viridian and quick cuckoos,
The orange-flashing parrots
Who retire as the sun falls down
In a sudden flare of tangerine.

Personal and cosmic now
Our way upon a mineral edge,
A hard grey narrow margin where
Sea and stone and bronze fuse
To merge in hot cyanine light.

From the sensual trade wind
Unannounced and lenient we
Depart for a perpetual void,
Where only ideas survive -
Always seeking knowledge.

As pelicans glide to further isles
Rays shoot upward from the sun,
Main and genoa are sheeted in
The vessel puts out from a cove
Entering the turbulence of streams.

Sometimes we change our shape
Are seen to recommence,
With endeavour and complexity
We resume and recur - the same
As we refine our vision.

Sea-bones, sea-wreckage, all
Remorselessly rejected,
Upon a carious rotten coast
Turning to fine sea-powder
For curving barren mangrove roots.

This smooth damp rim of earth
Forever without exertion,
Where sweat runs down and gathers
On a moist and silvery lip, stained
With turmeric and vanilla.

Through saline coriander skies
Meteors fall like sullen planets,
In apricot and turquoise evening
Cerulean clouds reveal their core
As sea and ocean clash and meet.

The ordered measure of a fan
Whose rotors cool a room,
Deep motors thrum far away
To navigate an opulent depth
Of the gigantic unperceived.

When our ship weighs anchor
Jib and staysail drawn tight,
The boat gently takes a course
Hesitating as we cross the flood
To go and meet with extinction.

A serum-coloured plosiveness
Of low and seamless dawn,
Where the islands turn cerise
As instantly the sloops tack out
Heading windward once again.

Who shall weigh our souls
When the sun retreats forever,
When the compass never points
And the bays are unremarked
Who shall patrol these islands?

As the form of waves travel
Extending throughout time,
So the ephemeral shall cause
Beauty to reside on earth -
Incessantly and lightly transient
As we are kind and just in love.

for Gregory Kallimanopoulos

I V - 2

THERE where the sea brooded and roared
That in ecstasy rolls back
And throws itself repeatedly
Threshing the sand for a single truth:

Dawn, slight blue before light becomes
Visible and mild to human eyes,
With distant lights of other islands
And far-off lamps of passing ships:

Stepped hills appear and trees
And a grey-mercury reeling ocean,
All the fiction of the earth, images
That we hold close to ourselves.

Then desire begins to swerve -
Ulesses wakening seeks his wife,
Caressing her about the hips
As they lie naked in the world.

He heard the vivid squalls passing
Drumming hands on their zinc roof,
And dozing in and out of sleep
He moved closer, alongside Kiki.

The indifference of unmoving Kiki
As she listened to the sea,
Prolific and profuse it seethed
Reaching, withdrawing repeatedly.

Gone were the lost mornings when
She would yield all her desire
To luxuriate in her husband's passion,
Those nights were no longer young.

Near to their little teak-wood house
Small coffee-coloured cows browsed
Along the black sand of the shore
White egrets perched upon their flanks.

She could smell the first smoke
Of day, odour of dung and grass,
And hear a thudding of boats
Noisily speeding across the swells.

A kingfisher chattered as it flew
Across the bay beneath their land,
As lunar shadows were stretching out
Upon the ground in tedious shapes.

Small anacondas coiled and knotted
The forest dripped with sweet rain,
Smoke hung acrid on leaves and air
Green-throated colibris and blossom.

She could hear the first motors
As boats dashed out towards the fields,
Doves and grackles pattered upon
The railings of their terrace:

The spray and boom of the sea
A final scattering of bats,
Mosquitoes hungry for human blood
Before the day caused them to vanish.

All these sounds reached Kiki's ears
As she lay still so as not to rouse
Her husband from the renewed sleep
To which he had once more descended.

So many years she had waited for him -
Ulesses working on the ships,
She never imagined a marriage defunct
That happiness could be so abandoned.

Another squall raced down from hills
Speckling the corrugated metal roof,
Then rushing slow explosions came
Of deep-grey pelting rainfall.

The couple rested on a thin bed
While black tarpon curled through the bay,
Arcing in perfect symmetry
Herding a shoal of darting fish.

She loved her husband - but now
His mood was speechless flint,
These days they scarcely spoke
Shared food together and casual loving.

She knew her devotion to be enduring
And like the rose of dawn he would
Always be there to accept her need,
But life had become an attendant waiting.

She loved Ulesses for his wandering reason
He had left the isle and returned,
Knew seas and iron islands and cities
Habits and knowledge, the skill of others.

Yet Kiki knew the magia of summons
Was familiar with spectral figures
Who appeared when her eyes were closed -
As fish touch a seam of water:

No longer capricious but clairvoyant
Kiki adored that limbo world,
Something she never admitted
Never mentioned to her husband.

His body smelled of salt and leaves
Of bread and oil - Ulesses,
This man who had once so ruled
Every second of her days.

Like an old cutlass now, he was
That hung upon a wall and rusted,
But their bound oaths of long ago
Remained perpetual for her.

There was a sound of pistons revving
Of plywood hulls striking waves,
A cry of male voices calling
Telling boats where the tarpon waited.

'What light shall burn away the suffering
Of painful grieving humanity,
What daring can release us,' she mused,
'From so much pity and duress?

This man I once imagined as
The perfect sum of all that breathed:
I gave myself to him because
He wanted me so much.

To me he taught compassion and
The timelessness of human spirit,
His foresight and accuracy
Were for me more than life.'

Through the doorway she could see
Rosy tips and strands of dawn,
Could hear the ferry's engines humming
Entering the bay it slowed its pace.

'This is the smallest day,' Ulesses
Had said as they retired last night,
'The sun is standing now and soon
Will move backward on the horizon north:

Like glossy planets in the sky at dusk
When the ghostly sea pauses,
As insects and gliding birds test
The flashing and shining darkness:

Then I know that soon we could
Be easily walking out of time,
Into the light beyond the hills
Beyond the ocean's ancient sounding.'

Kiki withdrew from bed and went
To stroll the grounds of their pasture,
Watching the sea, listening, waiting
For new promises to break her doubt.

A rimmed moon extinguished itself
Among dense marine clouds,
As the first pelicans swung on the air
She thought of her sleeping husband.

Untimed, impersonal, careless
Yet whole and benign: the vastness
Of nocturnal trade-wind soothed her
Its glittering heaven and sheer air.

Days were blurred and weightless now
Fused and simply indistinct,
They were like her grey-eyed husband
Pensive and involved of evening.

She was so tentative and Ulesses
So masculine and made of bones:
But no one lived in her amber eyes
Her soul was always ranging elsewhere.

It was Ulesses who gave her place
Stature and torso that she could hold,
And when he lay between her legs
She thrilled with her body's issue.

'Sometimes my soul goes to a dancing place
And alone and quite free
It plays and turns and watches there,
Yet soul has no memory – like Ulesses.

How all of life takes from us
Some days more, some days less,
Each dawn measures and subtracts
Reducing us as it rushes away.

The irony and paradox of life
Which only love can combat,
Love keeps our diminution
From removing us from this earth.

The world is animate and true
And we - a tissue-globe of thought,
One forceful the other insubstantial
And that is all that we can say.

Love gives us tongues and insight
It fills us with concupiscence,
Without love we are empty creatures
Phantoms who cannot speak nor touch.

His voice removed my loneliness
Just as his strength took my lust,
In his person I find a home
And in his sleep I find rest.

He is my snake and fruit-tree
He is the child I envisage,
And during the insensible night
He is the glow that reveals a man.'

A bright pink dawn was rising
And insects swarmed like birds,
And as the blue sea played turquoise
A white and molten moon was green.

The inside of her thighs were still
Wet from the hours before,
When Ulesses had woken at midnight
Compelling her satisfaction.

His scent and tang was on her skin
Her hair still tangled by
His passion and taut urgence,
A smell of kisses stayed in her mouth.

'True solitude,' he had once said,
'Occurs when the most restless element
Of a man's need to forget
Comes to rest in a woman's arms.'

He would always remain her match
Even if gravity and reserve
Made her discount a first tenderness
During the time when they were young.

Sea-grape and coco-palm nodded
As she looked out from the railing,
Recalling the anguish of his manner
When he had fallen asleep last night.

Kiki stood by her garden beside
The datura and okra and sorrel bush,
Something in her longed to weep
Some unspeakable desperation.

Trees, leopard-coloured in the dark
The moon ringed with tortoise-shell,
Under a net Ulesses lay sighing
And she longed for him and wept.

'Gone is the golden age when love
Was complete and men and women
Found neither emptiness nor despair
When vision was love's phase and source.

Now my unbearable soul is craving
And my husband is not a man
But a piece of cloth and a few buttons,
Like a fish with nothing to say.

Coco-palm,' she said, grasping the tree,
'I planted you when we married,
Now you grow and fruit and shake
And I am alone with a man's misery.'

She could hear the spiralling cry
Of cockerels' voices in the village,
The listless bark of a dog and
A bristling of night's last darkness.

'He dances in his masks and I
Dance in mine and at times
The music turns and we pass on the floor,
And sometimes our masks are the same.

That is all that love achieves -
A spontaneous recognition of person,
Features we wear in our oblivion
When soul possesses no view of its own.'

'I bear a great love for this place
But I know of no loyalty to location,
I have only my love for you,' he had said,
'And I fear to lose this island.

Despond and remorse give us hope
For without love we are void,
Silence is the most complete space
For those who have no home.'

'Have I wasted my youth,' she thought,
'Become another's courtesy,
Body whom he takes to himself
When he needs to lose his life?

The axle of our lives is hidden
We see the moon and sun and think -
Yes, this is how we turn,
Yet there is no turning of love's wheel.'

Once, his solitude had drawn her
But now his reticence was exceeding,
It was as if he were captive
To an idea or lost experience.

She loved to walk the grounds
During night when the stars shot
And crackled overhead and the moon
Was luminous on the ocean's surge.

In a shadowy stainless blackness
The passing and responsive flutterings
Rustling and footfall – all these
Were familiar powers to Kiki's mastery.

On the mountain-side nearby
An upright tall stone chimney
Of the old lime factory stood
Perpendicular and guardian:

Among many ruined citrus trees
And thorny bougainvillea bushes,
The genius of time - flawed and unfirm
Was like her husband's dreaming.

'How to love a man who is not there,
To watch him tap his barometer
And stand before a wooden idol
His hands folded in prayer?'

A meteor scorched and burned a track
Sparking downward from the sky,
She knew she must return to him
For often at dawn he needed her.

Snakes, bats, fireflies, these
Were her muted companions,
Goats, sheep, dogs, cattle
The donkeys, fowl, and the apparitions.

As she walked back up to the house
Masses of small brown mosquitoes
Touched and ran against her face,
Her feet slipping in the rain.

She loved the saline wind at night
Its sugary smoky warmth and how
It rushed upon her and against the sea
Driving waves onto sandstone rocks.

Curling back towards the bed
Beneath the silky net - she moved
Beside her husband whose immobility
In the darkness amazed her.

That day she would have to walk
Across the isle for a wedding,
In the boatyard where her godson
Was to accept a blonde-eyed girl.

She heard the weekly tanker drop
Its bronze anchor to the bay,
Ready to receive vessels whose engines
Needed fuel and news from the isles.

She recalled how she and Ulesses met
He had seduced her with tales
Of other domains, hardship and people,
She had been caught in his storied web:

'You are my ship called *Patience*
With your green mascara and azure glances,
Where youth and beauty mix like the sea
In a happy mist of mutual pleasure.'

The powdery jasmine-coloured sky
Coral and blue of alto-cirrus,
An oval moon occluded by cloud
As they walked home from the bar that night.

Kiki, solemn and distressed now
They slept on the veranda of the house,
Wanting so much the love of her husband
Yet tired of his habitual embrace.

Once he had laughed so much with her
They had walked the island for miles,
She had shown him all the paths
The sandy coves, bays and caverns:

They had loved so much in those years
Their ardour inhabited the isle,
Now their kisses were performed
Enacted without detail.

Yet she loved this turbulent surly man
His words were the walls of her heart,
To her, he was as much a presence
As the landscape of these shores.

Day released its milky haze
A humid blur of waves and light,
A quiet plosive rush of marine
Forever smoothing and filling the rocks.

Like an octopus explodes to blackness
With a sudden discharge of fear,
So Kiki dropped her shift to the floor
Slipped easily beside her naked man.

He was awake and touched her breasts
She sensed his fervent movement,
Then he was upon her and inside
And she forgot her disillusion:

As the sea crumpled on the shore
As iguanas rhythmically shook their heads,
As the coco-palm quivered with breeze
So Kiki felt her life return.

Her soul – like forest amaryllis
Rose upward and opened out its leaves,
As humming-birds hovered and alighted
A candescent heat imbued her blood.

His estranged soul approached at last
Its vibration rose in her tissue and cells,
Her body stirred like the ocean stirring
And with a final exhalation she cried:

All the pain, loneliness and sorrow
Experience that possessed no word,
Disappeared as his body rose and fell
And the implacable man she loved returned.

As her husband exclaimed his joy
And his limbs carefully relaxed,
Kiki felt his shoulder muscles
His fatigue and weariness loosely soften,
Each of them murmured the other's name.

I V - 3

'YOU, wakening in your soft white net
Smelling of sleep and sweet grapefruit,
   I long to taste your lips and drink
      The water only you possess.

   I love you for your body's light
   You are my motive being and rest,
      Vivacious, deliquescent, you
   Are the spirit of my new woman.

      I love your candid solitude
   The way you walk along the shore,
      Never swerving like the wind
      Completely like the darkness.

      I love your pity for all kind
   The trust you have for human speech,
   Compassionate with affection, you
      Apprehend love's transparency.

      I love your sensuous liberty
         The way you do not recall,
         I observe no consciousness
      Without your true compulsion.

You are the pain when I am beaten
         Replete with all anxiety,
      On double wings of grief I rise
      Toward your singular estate.

      Beautiful and soothing, you
   Are like a young traveller's tree,
      Within a subtlety of shadow
      You know how it is to love.

You expose to me love's tissue
So my thirst becomes fluid,
All that runs upon your tongue
About the smallness of your torso.

Citron-trees with wrens and swallows
Entangled in your topaz vision,
Revealing and mnemonic, you
Are my perfect absolution.

I love your ideal gentleness
Equilibrium of your wealth,
Yet how I suffer and endure
For my experience of you.

Like an octopus or starfish
Or an iridescent dolphin,
Something lucid in your eyes
Is never quiet nor still.

Agile, mobile, unhesitating
As we move together, coupled,
Two bloods flowing uniform
I hear the ocean in your voice.

A pang I feel throughout this life
Not being wholly at your side,
With you in my arms I am
United and so universal.

Briefly, I borrow you in time
Glimpsing through your living form,
Yet earthly vigilance is weak
And you evapourate.

The moon is settling into waves
And admiring her recession
You are the tawny bird whom
I touch with slow desire.

Mistress of my patience, you
Stand upon the many hours,
Like uprising cumuli
You come and go upon me.

In my mouth I taste your flesh
Your slightness and vitality,
I love the slippery sensitive
Currency of your passion.

My leeward and my windward place
Trade wind of all existence,
You are my three-masted boat -
Dare I name and announce
You mirror of the invisible?'

A TRUE GUIDE TO LOVE

EROS is a book that comes from travelling many years and four continents, from the Americas, to Europe, to Asia, and to Africa where all our myths and themes began: that original situation of *super*-nature and of paradise. The foundation of our cosmos rests upon this fabulous and ubiquitous congress of the male and feminine whose indelible unity and unapproachable resolution is perpetually ours to endure.

Just as a metal blade is tempered and made flexible and firm by immersion in fiery heat and cold water, so too are the human affections strengthened by grief and loss as much as by the act of loving and its arts. For if we grieve it is because we have loved, and if we love then we are destined to endure grief at some point in the future; this is simply the nature of earthly time. Tears are in this sense a pure sign of life and as part of the universe they touch lightly on our lives. For those who are fully aware there can be no expiration of either of these double emotions.

The book's narrative moves from a singular individual distinction toward the increasingly social and synoptic, for such is the nature of transition which occurs in the human psyche as it advances through the years and simultaneously recalls both the private and communal past. If love is the source of all our metaphors then consciousness can be only indicative and not real; the genius of lyric poetry pursues and represents this kindness of signification, identifying the patterns which texture and weave the heart through a contrary merging of metaphor and metonym, the warp and weft of temporal experience and pleasure.

Love of place, love of person and also, love that possesses no object, occur as dimensions here, each in their way generating further metaphors anew. It is only the love that holds or takes nothing as its object which sustains the most beautiful and wonderful fashioning of human alertness, an emotion that is actually timeless and perpetual: the kind of love to which any rite or liturgy aspires to approximate or to invoke.

Ultimately, if there are no entities then there exists only an arrangement of narratives that engage with each other and find continuity in the appearance of years. EROS at its most superlative is expressed by the amorous hero, that marginal figure who concentrates all experience in what—in terms of narrative—can be best described as our *eroica*: moving backward in time from the New World toward our original *locus* and forward in time from an illusively discrete solitude toward our full and common-wealth of human amity and exchange, always giving more than we receive.

INDEX OF FIRST LINES

Kevin McGRATH was born in southern China in 1951 and was educated in England and Scotland; he has lived and worked in France, Greece, and India. Presently he is an associate of the Department of South Asian Studies and poet in residence at Lowell House, Harvard University. Publications include, *Fame* (1995), *Lioness* (1998), *The Sanskrit Hero* (2004), *Stri* (2009), *Jaya* (2011), *Supernature* (2012), *Heroic Krsna* and *Eroica* (2013), *In The Kacch* and *Windward* (2015), *Arjuna Pandava* (2016), and *Raja Yudhisthira* (2017). McGrath lives in Cambridge, Massachusetts, with his family.

www.ingramcontent.com/pod-product-compliance
Lightning Source LLC
Chambersburg PA
CBHW030940090426
42737CB00007B/493